Diving into Ink

Poems of Love, Doubt, & Discovery
and
Lyrics from the Five Musicals

by Joe Ortiz

Early Lyrics Publishing

Early Lyrics Publishing—ASCAP
504 Bay Avenue
Capitola, CA 95010
Published by Capitola Gayle's, Inc.
Contact Information: Joe Ortiz: joe@gocapitola.com

This is a work of fiction. Names, characters, places, and incidents are prod-
ucts of the author's imagination or are used fictitiously. Any resemblance to
actual events or locales or persons, living or dead, is entirely coincidental.

Library of Congress Cataloging-in-Publication Data:
ISBN: 979-8-9891943-0-8

Diving into Ink—Poems of Love, Doubt, and Discovery
        and
Lyrics from the Five Musicals
Joe Ortiz

Cover design: Gayle Ortiz
Cover Photo: Anacortes, Joe Ortiz

Printed in the United States of America

2023

First Edition

Other books by Joe Ortiz

The Village Baker, 1993, Ten Speed Press

The Village Baker's Wife, co-authored with Gayle Ortiz and Louisa Beers, 1997, Ten Speed Press

Shakespeare on Golf, co-authored with John Tullius, 1997, Hyperion

The Gardener's Table, co-authored with Richard Merrill, 2000, Ten Speed Press

Four of the Poems appeared in the following publications:

The REED, San Jose State Literary Journal, 1969, "Poem Tree"

Mr. Toots Newsletter, 1989, "After Vallejo"

Mr. Toots Newsletter, 1989, "Between Storms"

Santa Cruz Sentinel, 1998, "Between Storms"

The Lyrics have been performed in the following productions:

BREAD!—The Musical: 2001-2017, Kuumbwa Jazz Center, Santa Cruz, Ca.
> The Black Bart Theater, Murphys, Ca.
> Shelton Theater, San Francisco, Ca., just to name a few.

SMOKE Cabaret: Numerous locations, 2001-2017, including:
> Tehama Country Club, Carmel-by-the-Sea, Ca.
> Kuumbwa Jazz Center, Santa Cruz, Ca.
> The RRAZZ Room at the Hotel Nikko, San Francisco, Ca.
> Shelton Theater, San Francisco, Ca.

Kitchen Kabaret dinner theater:
> 2004, Michael's On Main Restaurant, Soquel, Ca.

Escaping Queens: 2012 and 2013, Cabrillo Stage, Aptos, Ca.
> Queens Theater, 2014, Corona Park, N.Y.
> Hillbarn Theater, 2017, Foster City, Ca.
> Shelton Theater (concert reading), 2017, San Francisco, Ca.

Circus, 2019, Cabrillo Stage, Summer Festival, Aptos, Ca.

For MP3 recordings of songs and other literature by Joe Ortiz, visit: https://www.gaylesbakery.com/artwork-by-joe-ortiz/

Invocation

This is how I categorize
my life, in folders.

As the planet turns, and burns,
and smolders.

As humanity rants, and reels,
and rages:

This is how I chart
my life
. . . . on pages.

Dedication

For Gayle, the one and only

Table of Contents

The Poems

1) On Art, Writing, and Discovery

2) Love and Trust

3) Our Nature

Song Lyrics

Introduction

Having "grown up" in journalism in high school and junior college, then as an English major in college, I often found myself with a pen or pencil in hand; editing or revising became an obsession, usually indistinguishable from the task of writing itself.

Never wanting to commit to a life's work of either teaching or journalism, I aspired to become a writer. But what kind of future was that, I asked myself. In fact, I didn't have anything to write about—no stories per se, merely jokes, observations, anecdotes. "Irreverent correspondences" was what I called my contributions to conversation.

So, I floundered for many years, until I met my future wife, Gayle—the most important event of my life. As a law school dropout, I spent my time as a musician and discovered that the easiest way to make a living was as a house painter.

The house-painting paid the bills. But working as a musican was short lived, because I dreaded performing and carting equipment. So it didn't take long for me to decide to write musical theater pieces so I could express myself without having to be on stage. This was roughly in 1972.

There was only one problem: I had to develop my so-called "craft." I had taken creative writing and poetry courses at San Jose State, and studied Shakespeare and both the English and American novel. I was lucky to get published early on, but I didn't have any confidence. In fact, years later, when I published a poem in the Newsletter for Mr. Toots (the iconic café in Capitola Village), the bio read:

> Joe Ortiz gave up writing poetry in 1974 "in order to learn how to speak." Now he writes an occasional verse, convinced that, for him, mastering the art of speaking is impossible. Ortiz, co-owner of Gayle's Bakery, will publish a bread-baking book with Prentice Hall Press sometime this year. He also writes on restaurants for *The Sun*.

So, if I was going to write songs and theater pieces, I decided to write poetry for one full year to "practice" writing lyrics. Since then, I've learned that good things take time; nevertheless, devoting a full a year to my avocation was a leap of faith—never knowing if it would take hold.

That journey began roughly 50 years ago, when Gayle and I got married on the beach in San Francisco, in view of the windmills in Golden Gate Park—fitting symbols of my quixotic quest for self-expression.

The result is the book you hold in hand—the poems that shaped my early writing practice and led to writing songs. In the second section, you'll discover a few of my very favorite lyrics.

1. On Art, Writing, and Discovery

Diving into Ink
For Steve McGuirk at Huntington Lake

High on an alpine lake,
I stand on the floating dock as it squeaks
to the moon at midnight.
What an impulse I have
to enter the dark glass cathedral.

My toes grip at the frayed rug of the dock
at the edge of the world.
I hold fast in its gentle swaying,
frozen by the chill of glossy black ink
that dreads the nightmare of tumultuous sleep.

My mind, barren as a blank page,
glides on the glassy surface of memory.
My body, balanced like a pen over ebony paper,
screams with the invisible ink of intention
my darkest dreams of desire:
to etch between each star's reflection
on the lake the abstract lines
that will link them in some distant
constellation.

Harnessed by thought and safe
from emotion, I lunge
into the blackness,
    into ink—
Subterranean liquid madness, deafening silence,
unctuous coma of eternal blindness.

Here, there are no stars—
The moon is a forgotten memory
I leave my soul behind
on the creaking dock.

Two Ways

There are two
ways:

You can set out
with

A goal in mind
A path

Or you can set
out

With no plan
No

Map of inten-
tion

to guide you on to
see

A way to move for-
ward.

This latter plan
is

One of discovery
With-

in this brave task
you

Uncover the
path—

Haphazard as you
go—

with attention
to

how the pattern un-
folds

How the road
swerves

which you
follow

or get hopelessly
lost

and search in faith,
until

an answer reveals
itself or an-

other question
asked.

Knitting on Canvas

For Kaffe and Holly, brother and sister, who belong to the Fassett family.

This wild and creative clan of artists and makers has run Nepenthe on the Big Sur Coast since their parents bought the property—then a rustic home— from Orson Welles in 1947 and eventually turned it into a restaurant. Family lore says that Holly taught Kaffe (world famous knitting designer) how to knit. They now paint in oil, acrylic, and watercolor, both separately and together, in Greece and London and on the Big Sur Coast. Someday I'll learn the story of how and why they named the gift shop below the restaurant THE PHOE-NIX. For now I'll remain content in the fascination of that mystery.

1.
In the morning during toast & coffee
you knit while I arrange lines on paper,
contours with charcoal on cardboard   knots
in swatches   diagrams charted to uncover
some secret.
   The surface
of the marble table   decked
with coffee stain and crumb   reflects
the loop your wrist makes   the flip
& twirl of needles   the tattered
ends of yarn like nerve endings
that shock the brain into pattern—
design. From your mind
      to mine.

2.
From this,
our fashion rises
out of ashes   from a family loud
with fire   smoke & silence   wild
with the threads that tie the unspeakable
into story   into yarn
of color   quilted patchwork texture
— your craft & mine—
    designed to cover us.

3.

      You shape a still life
for me out of color from your palette
out of vase & fabric   like the skeins
you pick for strangers off a yarn-shop
shelf for a sweater. You hand me a brush
& say paint.

     Lost in your spatial
arrangement   hypnotized by shape
far from the dark cabin above Nepenthe
I still hear voices from the café   words
like stitches
     I see images crackling
from the bonfire   yarns dancing
like brushstrokes
          Encrusted party cakes
pattern-on-pattern   books arranged
by color
colored bottles plastered
together as walls   portraits of our past
covered in dust.
         The bag of bright red apples
one for each face of a half-dozen children
perched like hungry birds at the window
for the Big Sur crowd to ponder.

Mother's quilted bed   Father's woolen voice
like a thread   that ties us to desire
your heart and mine.

4.
I close my eyes & see the blue Delft tiles
you painted by hand   made to match
the existing   commissions   the infamous
& gaudy red flowered mural painted over
by a client crazier than you were
minutes after you laid the final brush stroke.

I think of your vermillion spirit
lying under six layers of monotone   pastel
decorator white   your burning pentimento
of fire that tugs us back to the stories
once told in the cabin   under blankets
your yarns & mine.

5.
I want to paint
a persimmon   draw a line that shapes
a pear   knit the angle of your wit
fashion contours of a fig   nestle cantaloupe
next to aubergine   dream a still life
alive as you would   with placement
color   to gather a swatch of wit
& swirl of landscape   the knit & purl
of surface
        To paint a palm tree of teal
turquoise chairs against cerulean walls
in a café on Lesbos   color   holler
with shape & edge
next to edge   without line

        Triangles
turning into pears   squares next
to squares   shifting into plums
in shades of mauve   magenta   cabernet
the color of straw   a field   wild grasses
your light   shimmering off the surface
of a garment
            painted stitches.

6.
My finger feels the tug
to follow
the invisible
shape of your soul,
to trace
the impossible
edge of your design

My hands long
to dig into your infinite
colored earth   tone blanket

My mind
to languish
in the liquid amnesia
of your water-
        color
solution

To go down
Deep beneath
The still-life
pattern
of your surface
                Into the depths

You   mine.

This is How I Chart My Life

This is how I chart my life
on pages
while humanity rails and rants
and rages

While the human race
runs & sacks & stages
passion plays designed
to last the ages

This is how I stack beliefs
In mounds and batches,
categorize my thoughts—
strike my dreams with matches

While hectic human life engages
in the noble task
of earning wages
I beg ideas to hide

Inside, tucked away in folders
while the planet turns
and yearns and burns and smolders.

This is how
I chart my life.

2. Love and Trust

Sister, Mother,
   Lover, Wife
Haleakala, Maui, 9-1-96

Last night I watched you
sleeping. I felt your body rise
and stall.
I wanted to touch you
without your waking.
   I remembered
how we shifted in the darkness
one night and fumbled to
clutch one another's hand.
         This distance makes
me want to circle around you,
hover above you, travel great
distances so I can return.

If I could carry you on my
      shoulders
through the desert looking for
            water

If I could tie a silken thread
around your wrist
and the other end to my own
wrist

If I could see your face again
in the garden
when you said, I will do
everything I can to help you

And if at that moment
I could have ravished you in
my arms and penetrated your
spirit—
      (huddled in one another's
         arms, weeping)

Our bodies melding into lava from
      our fire
into ashes on the burning lawn

And if the sediment of rivers
      could have covered us in a bed
      of alluvium
      and our souls be fused after
      a thousand years
      into a crystal gem—

Then I would know that I could say
I love you
      without speaking

And touch you in the night
without your waking, and find
myself lost in the rise and fall
of your breath.

When Eve First Blushed

When Eve first blushed
All our bouts with fear began.

There on the stage,
her encores came quickly
Her arms snuggled comely
To cover the creases
We already knew she had.

Dig the Fig - Birthday Poem

I dig the fig in you
I reach for
the peach
I crave
the nav-
el orange, I do
I grapple
with the apple.

Sublime
as the lime,
You are true . . .
Do I dare to
eat a pear?
When only a lemon
Will do?

Happy Birthday.
Stay
as fruitful as you are . . .

The Promise

Deetjen's – Big Sur, 16 June 1973

A solitary voice within
speaks of doubt
a solitary object
out of reach.

The voice of conception grows
out of the quiet body, from the need
to create something beyond the self:
the design, the child who will appear—
not as planned—yet still affirming
to the spirit what the blood has always known—
the birth.

The voice begins to be heard.
It springs from a common mouth.
Slowly it wanes as the mouth weakens.
Forgetting its birthright
it is silent, lost.

In this vast silence
the weight of no sound creates
a sad music, a song of faith through suffering—
to assure the forward going of the spirit.

Love, it says. But it asks, again
Which way to go? The voice of agreement
tells us we are onto something
good and everlasting, opening
new areas, a new age. But always letting go.

In the end, it is the shrill voice of the north,
careening down and out of the cold hills,
into our lives at the close of day—
stirring encounters,
freezing life for a moment of belief,
then sending it casually on its way.

3. On Nature

Every Night

Every night before I go to sleep
I imagine myself as a creature
in the forest flossing my teeth
on a pine needle.

In cohabitation
with rocks and stones and fallen branches,
I am part of the landscape,
leaning toward sky and sun with yearning

for respite from hunger and thirst
and constant searching
while dreaming each world alive—

I can only dream in the images
I hold before me—only in the rocks
& cliffs & sky, the stream of sudden passing,

the interminable migrations,
the kinship of life-sharing
creatures like myself who know
nothing but what we know.

Between Storms
Stockton Bridge, January 1997

The waves roll under the pier
& pilings shudder. The river runs
out through the beach—a mouth of sand—
    and quibbles with the sea.
Brown water meets brown water.
Waves that started out on a mountain
    above Loma Prieta
meet waves that began in a place
    beyond El Niño

Two boys
launch driftwood as boats and follow
the vessels down until they maroon
on branches.
    They kick them loose
    and out to sea.
There is no lack of wood for their imaginings,
no lack of current for setting their hopes
    adrift.

When they tire of embarkations & navigations,
they throw rocks, kick sand, chase seagulls,
take turns dragging logs bigger than they are,
    rolling others using poles as fulcrums,
until their desire to set a sodden log adrift
outweighs its own ability to float.

Poem Tree

Out of context,
in a flattened landscape
the bending shape
is still in evidence.
One can sense
a former intercourse
of branches
from which an order
seemed to grow.

Here it stands
in the field,
yet still under
the shadow
of the old oak
once on the hill
but now long fallen.

The Vow

For Rex Ranger

To wit, to wit:
the cigarette.

The prosecution
never rests.

I do feel guilt
and live with it.

The State
has pointed out, indeed,

it knows I need
those things I hate.

It locks me up
for what I hold

in hand, knowing
I who live in crime

will never judge myself
by what I quit.

A little more of it
becomes me. Testify?

Take the stand?
Swear to it?

Yes, I can walk the line,
distinguish right from wrong
as anyone can do.
Never touch another smoke.

It is the only way,
it's true.

But comfort too
was once a vice,

(though now I wear it
round the waist

as well as
baggy flannel shirts

that hold me
to a comforting fit.)

So, leave me
in my state.

I cannot move an inch
to get away from it.

Tobacco.
I know!

I only use it
by the pinch.

What is Water to Me

i.
I try
to describe
it

It comes out
only
in words.

The land breathes
sea
at rivermouth

the flight
below,
above my sight

of birds.

ii.
I sat
at the ocean
alone.
And it was
all, and
it was
nothing.

iii.
In the rose
lies
the reason

petals fall,
seeds will rise
like birds

in flight
beneath
spring rain.

Words bring
pain.
Tomorrow

Forever diving
sparrows
sing.

After Vallejo

¡Dare not open the eyes!
The world is what it is.
But pictures on the eyelids, dreams,
define the shapes of our refusals.

My mother sits in darkness, weeping.
My father rides in the depths of God's night.
They must know objects, situations, circumstance.

¡Dare not give to pain what it asks in return!
We blame our situations for our griefs,
the past for what we suffer now.
We call this pain most grave.
We will sit in darkness praying for light.
We will see blossoms burning,
feel black minions in the blood
and know a thousand nameless griefs
before the light returns.

In this I fall to sleep,
remain inside—remain.

I think of coming out,
I often think of the power
of the mind to turn the blood,
reshape the heart to its own image.
¡And what an image that is!

I am thinking of wide, strong light—
awakening to the sea, the possibility of shapes
that are new, the bright object . . .
simplicity of surfaces.

I dwell in the bright, white shadows
of situation. Such are the dreams
of circumstance.

Song Lyrics from the Five Musicals

Songs from *Kitchen Kabaret* at Michael's on Main

In nine months of Thursday-night shows in 2001, I spearheaded a band of local entertainers in running dinner-theater performances at Michael's on Main in Soquel, starring (among many others) Lori Rivera, Juni Bucher, Durage Maxfield, Rick McKee, and Katie McKee, with Art Alm on piano and Steve Larkin on bass. We offered dinner and a show for $28 in an intimate private room, seating 60 guests.

Greg Fritsch, my long-time director, script collaborator, and former waiter and maître d', set up the seating and supplied carefully-placed clip lights on a dimmer switch to add a theatrical feeling to the performance. But Greg's greatest contribution, besides directing each theatrical segment, was to suggest the unfolding of the evening's presentations: three mini-acts, each of twenty minutes' duration between courses of the meal.

As guests arrive, the band plays jazz arrangements from the show. At the proper moment, the band exits to applause and the salad course is served.

When the plates are cleared, lights go up on stage, the band reenters, and the first "salad-course" musical skit takes place. After fifteen minutes of song, theater, and applause, the actors and band exit and the "main dinner course" is served. And once again, the audience enjoys the headline entertainment, and the "dessert course" is served, and quickly thereafter, the Finale, featuring all entertainers in one last "curtain call" of an original Ortiz composition from the evening's show.

The Master of Ceremonies Introduces the Show

In a mixture of what I call "Circus Music & Carnival Magic," an odd little musical ditty popped into my head, helping to lend a strange and eerie vibe over the performance. The song "Ragu" was sung at different times by Rick McKee and Glen Rose, each acting as the emcee, in introducing the audience to what we hoped was a bizarre and unique evening of entertainment.

"Ragout"

RAGOUT of little lies
of sauce and fancy
Superstition stew
Salad of remorses
Yearning served in four courses
Wishes delicious
A passionate brew

You'll crave our little pies
Be brave and taste them
Eat and get your fill
Dishes of defenses
Soup of our six senses
Side-dish of anguish
To cure every ill

Now taste a little bite
Of that which ails you
Feed the savage beast
Agonies you borrow
One last sip of your sorrow
There's no tomorrow
So, savor the feast

Tell me what you want
We'll give you what you need
A bitter taste to taunt
Blind faith on which to feed.

So, smile and sing
Don't cry or think
The sauce will never heal
What you refuse to feel
Lift hand to mouth
And eat and drink
So, joy can be a part of the deal

Yes, smile and sing
Don't cry or think
The sauce will never show
What we're afraid to know
Yes, hurry up
And eat and drink
So we can get
On with the show!!!!

Songs from *BREAD!—The Musical*

BREAD!—The Musical, a semi-autobiographical story about a baker who, both figuratively and literally, gets stoned on his own bread, was produced in many manifestations and venues starting in 2001: The Santa Cruz Yacht Club, Bocci's Cellar, Avanti Restaurant, Black's Beach Café, Café Lido, Kuumbwa Jazz Center, Carl Cherry Theater (in Carmel), Black Bart Theater (in Murphy's, Ca.), COPIA—The Center for the American Institute of Wine and Food (in Napa), and in 2017 at Shelton Theater, starring Lori Rivera, Max Bennett-Parker, and Kim Larsen, with a brand-new script by Kathryn Chetkovich.

Actors during the 20 years of productions included Jonathan Arthur, Stacy Aronovici, Bruce Burns, Burr Nisson, Loren Creager, Dori Nolan, John Newkirk, Alice Hughes, Penny Hanna, Chris Grube, Frank Widman, Martha Rabin, Sara Wilbourne, Dohn Grube, and Spike Wong, to mention a few.

Musicians included Emiko Hayashi, Steve Larkin, Rebecca Coupe Franks, Dave MacGillicuddy, and Dan Robbins, among others.

Script doctors: Ralph Peduto, Greg Fritsch, Kathryn Chetkovich. Stage Managers: Bonnie Ronzio and Jim McCunn. Directors: Greg Fritsch and Katherine Adkins.

By far the funniest incident (and there were many) was when Jonathan Arthur—in the true spirit of a baker who was "under the influence" and unable to remember the words—wrote the lyrics to the song "The Perfect Loaf of Bread" on a three-by-five card taped to the live baguette prop he held as he sang the tune.

My Obsession With a Fresh Loaf Comes Out in Song!

I was lucky there was no mic and public address system the evening I was asked to sing this song at a meeting of the Bakers Guild of America, when one well-meaning member—having heard I'd written a song entitled "Bread!"— decided to wheel out a battered upright piano to encourage this shy, ill-prepared baker-turned-composer to sing for his supper.

Fortunately, no one could hear how I garbled the lyrics. However, they all applauded and for good reason: all of them being bread bakers, I'm sure they must have heard me barking out the word "bread" many times. If asked now to sing the song a capella, I'm sure I could do it, but at that time, playing it on piano while singing was a true challenge.

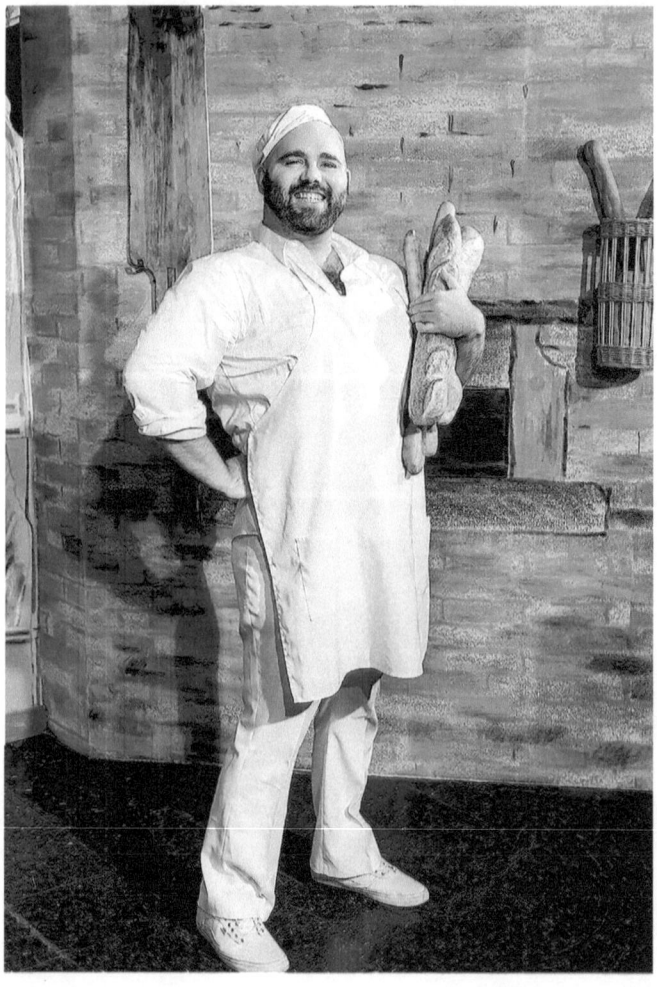

Max Bennett-Parker as Henri, the mad baker, in *BREAD!* at Shelton Theater, 2017

"Bread!"

Bread! . . . It's a sop for your soup
A way to recoup
The sauce on your plate
A way to relate to a stew

How would you
Handle a *pot au feu*
Without bread
What would *bouillabaisse* be
Could you serve ham and brie
It's something I seriously doubt you could do
without Bread

You'd be lost in a meal with no feel.
Can a finger and thumb
Serve better than crust or crumb
To get food to your mouth?
How could we . . . go picnicking under a tree
without bread?

Would a steak and *pommes frites*
Be considered good eats
Without just a hunk of baguette?

A jug of wine and some cheese
and thou beside me under trees
Saucisson and *charcuteries*
Bread! Bread! Bread! Bread!

Take bread! Make bread! Break bread!
For goodness sake, Bread!

Crackers would absolutely never, never do
With a *steak au jus* . . .
You need Bread!   Bread!   Bread!   Bread!

A hunk of bread . . . A little cheese
A glass of wine . . . And thou beside me under trees

And if you please . . . make mine . . . Bread!

The Dangerous Mind of a Baker Obsessed by Bread!

I borrowed the title "Damage and Desire" from a fellow playwright, Kate Ryan, whose play Leaving Queens *was yet to nail down a production. At the time, another play of Kate's, entitled* Damage & Desire, *was in readings in New York, so I asked her if I could write a song to see if she might be willing to put it in the show. When I played the finished version of my new composition for Kate she admitted she liked it but that was as far as it went.*

As is sometimes the case, the song fit nicely into another show. In BREAD!—The Musical *it worked, word for word, as a warning by the health inspector, who constantly harassed Henri, the mad baker, about removing all tainted rye grain from his boulangerie.*

The song became a big hit when Kathryn Adkins performed her sultry arrangement as the Health Inspector in an early production at Bocci's Cellar in Santa Cruz.

"Damage and Desire"

You walk a tightrope dance
Juggling trickery and trust
You dare to take a chance
So you leap because you must.
You fall through space with no regret
Without a trace of loss or threat
You'll ache, you'll bleed,
I'll make you heed
the lesson you require.
If you can't stand the height
Come on down from the wire.

Someday your dream will douse the light
Linking DAMAGE AND DESIRE

These incendiary games
Stoke the flair of passion's fire
You nurse a hungering for trust,
But you're famished by desire.
For you to know your scheme of lust
You must forego your dream of trust
You dwell within a game
Where joy and agony conspire.
If you can't stand the heat,
Back away from the fire

Your passion tasting bittersweet,
Mixing DAMAGE AND DESIRE.

A Maniacal Baker Fumes About Toast

I love argument songs—some bit of insanity a director can use to intensify the drama of a relationship.

As a passionate baker—admittedly crazed by inhaling sourdough fumes all day—I become enraged when anyone wants to toast a loaf that comes straight from the oven. By now you may have already figured that the story of Henri, the mad baker, is largely autobiographical. Something can snap when we become maniacally influenced by those aromas. We become obsessed by the hubris of creating some bit of personal invention to offer people to feed their souls (but admittedly, also to fuel our own egos when clients praise our offerings). Anyone in food preparation seems to possess this need for acceptance.

So, when someone wants to slice and toast a freshly baked loaf straight from the oven without even sampling its aroma, it brings out the beast in us.

Toast! *(sung in call and response);*

JOSETTE:
Just listen to me and never agree
To say the word around him . . . .

> HENRI:
> It makes me crazy

JOSETTE:
It makes me hungry
It goes with coffee
To start my day
Whenever the subject arises, I think,
He's ready to snap, he's on the brink . . . .

> HENRI:
> Whenever I hear the toaster click

JOSETTE:
It stirs my heart . . . .

> HENRI
> It makes me sick
> An honest hunk of fresh baked bread
> So, you can smell and taste
> The grain the most—TOAST!
> Tear bread . . . bare bread
> not cooked twice

JOSETTE:
Not even in a slice?

HENRI:
Simply simple, plainly plain
So you can clearly taste the grain
The way the almighty grew it
And the baker vows to see to it
No need for TOAST!
Whenever I smell the terrible scent
of bread that's burning

JOSETTE:
It makes me hungry . . . .

HENRI
To me it's blasphemy!
Insult to crumb and crust
Some people think they must
Take a loaf that's perfectly prized
Slice it and toast it
Until it's disguised
Ruin a marvelous hunk of bread
That's perfectly nice . . .
By cooking it twice!

The silly sound assaults my ears

JOSETTE:
Nearly bringing him to tears
A noise he fears . . . .

HENRI:
It grinds my gears.

JOSETTE:
Whenever he hears
The crackling sound of
Burning crust . . . .

HENRI
Some people think they must
Take a loaf that's perfectly prized
Soak it in butter until it's disguised
Ruin a marvelous hunk of bread
That's simply the most

JOSETTE
By making it . . . TOAST? . . . .

HENRI
TOAST!!

High as a Kite on Sourdough Fumes

The entire BREAD! *musical is in homage to the classic story, book, and movie by Marcel Pagnol,* The Baker's Wife.

Certainly, Steven Schwartz had already written his version, The Baker's Wife, *which appeared on Broadway in 1989, but my version was from the point of view of a working baker who not only knew the territory but also was known to get high on his own starter and fermented rye loaf.*

Since Gayle had several times complained of having gotten stoned on our rye bread, the "germ" was set in my mind. And a mind stoned on sourdough can only lead to fabulation—sailing off like a "Kite in the Wind."

"Kite in the Wind"

JOSETTE *(spoken)*:   Oh, Henri. How can I save you now?

(She sings.)

KITE IN THE WIND, I say good-bye
Float like a bird upon the wing
You bob and dive and come alive
Each time I pull the string
When I let go you'll sail away and fly

Bird, understand I let you go
Open my hand, I toss you to the sky.
When I deny my yearning,
I refuse to say goodbye
If I can't let you go,
We'll never know

     Melody, come back to me,
     Return to me
     Mem'ry like a string tied to my heart
     Will you feel the pull of my heart soon,
     Like the moon that pulls the ocean
     Tugging you right back to me
     Where you ought to be

Climb like a breeze through tall trees
Sway with my sadness when I cry
My soul believes the dancing leaves
Are echoing your goodbye.
Unless I let you go,
I'll never know if you can fly.

KITE IN THE WIND,
I say goodbye.

To Imagine is Celestial, to Hallucinate—Divine.

Most artists seem to repeat themes, concepts, and story lines.

I must admit, the songs "Electrify Me" and "Intoxicate Me" (to come later) and "You Hallucinate Me" follow similar verbal images for me.

The song "You Hallucinate Me" helped convey an important plot point in BREAD!, revealing how Henri, our mad baker—stoned on his own mind-altering sourdough starter and magical bread—was not only experiencing hallucinations of dancing baguettes but even visually manufacturing his wife's image.

I think the tune sums up what many of us might experience in our idolization of a love object. We see what we want to see. For this tune, I left in some of the stage direction so readers can see how the song took place in Greg's deft portrayal of the scene.

"You Hallucinate Me"

JOSETTE:
(She sings.)
Am I real? Maybe not
Can you deal with what
You've wrought?
Will I be . . . what you thought?
Can you see
If you love or hate me?

HENRI *(spoken)*:
I was trying to make
the perfect woman.
And it is you!

JOSETTE
Shall I go? Should I stay?
Do you know . . . I'm away?
I feel oh . . . so lost today
Though you're blind
YOU HALLUCINATE ME.

HENRI *(spoken)*:
Ma petite beignet.
It was always you.

JOSETTE:
Am I flesh? Am I bone?
Or am I fresh-
ly molded stone?

(They dance.)

You paint me in solid tone
From thin air you duplicate me
Rushing blood through my veins
Blooming bud, passion reigns
Roiling sea . The shore restrains
C'est mon affaire
YOU HALLUCINATE ME

*(Unbeknownst to HENRI,
CARLOTTA, still at the edge of
the stage removes her huge shawl,
revealing a smaller one under-
neath. It really is her, and not a
ghost. And she was there all along?
She leaves her cane behind and
begins to walk toward HENRI,
who remains unaware of her.)*

JOSETTE:
I become substantial in your sight
Just a glance from you and it might
    prove me
There's a chance some
circumstantial evidence
might cast a light to . . .

*(CARLOTTA, standing right
behind him now, sings the final
lines in JOSETTE's clear voice.)*

JOSETTE:
. . . Move me . . . groove me
Mold me . . . hold me

*(HENRI can't believe what he's
hearing. He turns and sees CAR-
LOTTA. But that voice—! As
she sings, she removes her shawl
and wig, revealing: JOSETTE.)*

Am I more . . . Am I less
You adore . . . What you obsess
Can I be your worthiness?
If you do . . .
HALLUCINATE ME?

Songs From *SMOKE*

SMOKE grew out of many shows we did at Michael's on Main in 2004. Having to come up with a new show every few weeks kept our creative team inventing new story sketches based on several core tunes—and a few new numbers that came from out of nowhere exactly when needed. The original *SMOKE* sketch was twenty minutes long, with a libretto written by Kathryn Chetkovich, first given life in a one-night fund-raiser at Broadway Theater months before the Michael's run began.

The concept was simple: "Imagine meeting a woman in a bar who starts telling you about her love life . . . in song!"

The story concept inspired three separate shows, each of 15 minutes' duration: the original, starring Lori Rivera; the variation, *Smoke Rings*, starring Juni Bucher; and the male companion piece, *Blowing Smoke*, starring Durage Maxfield. Originally all shows ran on separate nights.

The good fortune of frequently having to come up with new shows inspired us to run all three in one "smoke-filled" evening. When we finally had to call the nine-month Michael's run a wrap (exhaustion had set in), the brand-new *SMOKE* story came along with us to new productions in an hour-long script by Ms. Chetkovich. We still regard it as our most successful show and longest-running production—now approaching 20 years.

Sun and Shade Inspired

I remember the very day I came up with the title and hook for "Warm in the Sun." In 1971, on my short walk to Hastings Law School on an unseasonably hot, sultry day in San Francisco, where the only relief was in the shade of the Civic Center skyscrapers, I came up with the title "Warm in the Sun, Cool in the Shade." I kept the title in my brain until a year or so later, when I met Gayle in San Jose. The rest of the lyric wrote itself from my infatuation with this woman—my future wife—who came in and changed my life for good. I wrote the music while riding shotgun in my friend Howard's 1953 yellow Chevy convertible—battered guitar in hand—as he drove us down the 280 freeway on our way to connect with Gayle on another brilliant California afternoon.

"Warm in the Sun"

WARM IN THE SUN
COOL IN THE SHADE
Living together in fun
In love that we made
The sun through the trees
The streams where we played
WARM IN THE SUN
COOL IN THE SHADE

Who could believe
It's perfect like this?
As if it were made
For you and for me
A paradise where we
Can see what love is
What fun!
When it's
WARM IN THE SUN
COOL IN THE SHADE

I never had my hopes way up so high
I sang my early jokes
That perfect love could never be
I couldn't believe my eyes
But now I see . . .

This paradise, what fun
And all the love that we made
When it's
WARM IN THE SUN AND COOL . . .
WARM IN THE SUN, COOL . . .
WARM IN THE SUN, COOL IN THE SHADE

"If a show goes bust, throw the song into a new musical."

The song "Wind Me Up" was originally written for a musical play that never got written or produced.

The new, projected theater piece was to be based on a ten-minute play entitled The Barbies, written by Linnet Harlan who lived in Pacific Grove. Ms. Harlan's original, non-musical piece was performed as part of the Eight Tens at Eight Festival sponsored by Santa Cruz Actors Theater, but also published in Thirty 10-Minute Plays from the Santa Cruz Festivals I-VI (2001), a book containing the first six years of that competition's winning productions.

For some reason Ms. Harlan pulled out of our agreement to turn the show into a musical. So, I put the seven tunes I'd written into a folder and forgot about them.

Having been a musical theater buff for years, I'd learned by studying songwriting geniuses like Irving Berlin and Rogers and Hart that when the original show goes bust by closing early or never getting staged, composers would recast the lyrics and throw the tune into another production. (From what I remember, Berlin's song "Easter Parade" was one such tune.)

A decade later, "Wind Me Up"—with its allusions to smoldering passion and fire—found a perfect home in SMOKE Cabaret starring Lori Rivera.

As the strange world of musical theater would have it, the song may have yet a new life—oddly enough—in a new rendition of that original BARBIES concept, with a new title and a new script by Steve Spike Wong, a longtime friend and local playwright. Watch for it. As we say in the biz, "fingers crossed" in hopes for the success of a new production. PS: In the original show, the song was to be sung by Bad Barbie.

Of course, when the new Barbie Movie came out to great fanfare, I refused to see it until we had our original story fully mapped out. And I'm glad I did, for our show covers vastly different territory.

"Wind Me Up"

WIND ME UP
I can walk
I can do most anything
It's all about intention.
Do you know who I am?
I'm Smoke . . . Desire . . . Fire
Sister of invention

I will put make up on
Wear my heart for all to see
Forget my smart surprises
Do you know who I can be?
Starlight . . . A shadow . . . Moonbeams
Mistress of disguises

    I'll put my head in the mouth of the lion
    I'll walk the tightrope wire
    Fly the trapeze without any net
    I'll swallow swords and walk on fire

Dress me up (so) I can play
Any part you write for me
Master of my yearning
All too wise in disguise
I'm Smoke . . . Desire . . . Fire
Yes, inside I'm burning.

"Up All Night, Such a Thrill"

Sometimes odd title ideas slip into one's brain and get stuck there because they sound interesting, unique, or compelling. I don't know when or where the line "Oysters Any Time of the Day" came to me. But it sounded fascinating. And I can't recall why I thought a three-syllable line would be an interesting metric apparatus to use. Maybe it was because the first phrase, "Up at noon," arrived in a flash. And my obsession with prosody forced me to follow the pattern.

I believe Gayle had seen the show perhaps fifteen times when, on the street one day in San Francisco, she looked at me and said, "I just realized what the song is all about." She never told me what she thought. She just smiled. And I knew she knew.

Oysters Anytime of the Day

2003 ©

"Oysters Any Time
of the Day"

Up at noon
Dressed by three
Breakfast on
The balcony
Caviar
Dry champagne
It's who we are
Why complain?

Now you're gone.
So (it's) back to bed.
Thoughts of you
Run through my head.
A lazy snooze
All afternoon
My only care
What shoes to wear.

Here we go
Again tonight
I'll take you in
My soul's delight
What a life
O, how we play
Never mind
What people say

Up all night
Such a thrill
What we do
To get our fill
Let it slide
So sublime
OYSTERS ANY TIME
OF THE DAY

Love to feel
That satin silver
Slowly sliding down
So sublime, anytime

You'll take me
My little beast
What a spree
Such a feast
We'll both taste
Eternity
Oysters so sublime
And come what may
OYSTERS ANY TIME
OF THE DAY

A Mood of Melancholy and Longing

Gayle and I had just arrived home from a trip to Lisbon. Not only had we visited the Fado *Museum, but we'd taken in several late-night* fado *performances starring both male and female singers.*

The emphasis of fado *music—a mixture of flamenco and Spanish "folklorico," accompanied by the magical sound of Portuguese steel-string guitars—creates an emotional feeling the Portuguese call* saudade, *which means sadness, melancholy, nostalgia, or longing.*

The music's expression of intense emotion, often in a minor key, seems to help re-create the mood we needed for that plot point in SMOKE.

"Mister X – *(I Sat Alone Last Night)*"

I SAT ALONE LAST NIGHT
Sorting out my life as best I could
In walks a stranger –
Just a hint of bad and good
"Leave it alone," is what I said.

Have you seen Mister X?
Who leaves his effects
On the night table
When he goes?
He pays only his respects

There in the wee small hours
Alone in the dark
I saw him wink and look away
We shared a little drink
To honor what the moment brings:
No names, no hopes, no strings.

Small talk and repartee
A tender story to save the day
No hope and no regrets
And I was set to greet him halfway.

We lingered on to my place (No, never his),
And there on the pathway
He took me in his arms
He smothered me with bliss
And lost me in his charms
It was just a kiss
But, O, what a kiss can do . . .

O, what a kiss can do
To summon up those sublime effects
No hopes and no regrets
Have you seen Mr. X?

And I lose myself to the night
Intoxication leads to the celebration
I see my soul in flight
No care for tomorrow
Not a drop of sorrow I will ever know, no, no no, no . . .
Just the causes and effects of Mister X.

I SAT ALONE LAST NIGHT.

A Litany of Clichés

I got the title "What the Hell Happens to Love?" from a book published in the 1980s. It has always been said that you can't copyright a title, so I thought I'd used it for a cabaret song. The song came later in the twenty-year production history of SMOKE—after Kathryn Chetkovich wrote the final and current book.

I thought this provocative title as a hook would be an apt sentiment to express unrequited love.

When I wrote the first line, I said to myself, "Interesting, that sounds like a cliché." But I marshalled on, thinking, "Hey, I can delete that line after I get the entire lyric fleshed out." But then along came the second line, a cliché as well. So, it made me think, "Well, why not follow the 'in-your-face' attitude of cabaret by attempting to write a lyric composed completely of clichés?"

And here you have it. A woman who is so distraught about losing a loved one that she is forced to expresses herself in poetic absurdity.

In an early rehearsal of the song, Rebecca Coupe Franks came up with the chord progression that made the penultimate lyric line work to dramatic effect. And it stuck.

Before Lori took the song over as her own in SMOKE, Juni Bucher sang it in her companion solo show Smoke Rings. It was Juni who improvised the final line. And that stuck too. Today it remains an essential sentiment and fitting ending for the song.

"What the Hell Happens to Love?"

You wrapped your web around me
You caught me in your spell
Your loving arrow found my heart
And suddenly I fell
My knees went weak, I couldn't speak
The sky fell from above
What happened, what the hell happened?

You whispered softly in my ear
You wrung me like a bell
You dished up thoughts so strange and queer
My secrets I would tell
You had your way with me my dear
I lost the meaning of . . . what happened?
WHAT THE HELL HAPPENS TO LOVE?

> Love is the game we make up
> Why does it seem we always wake up?
> Love is a dream forsaken
> Why does it seem we must awaken?

You gave me hope but warned me
My future not to sell
We talked about eternity,
Tomorrow who could tell?
We'd crash and burn
And pray to learn
The tragic lesson of
What happened?
What the hell became of?
Oh, what?   What in heaven's name, love.
WHAT THE HELL HAPPENS TO LOVE?
(Improvised and partly spoken):
Won't somebody tell me?

"It got so hot, we put the fire out."

Greg and I were looking for a breakup song and "We Took It Off the Menu" fit the bill.

It was inspired by a statement made by a friend, George Germon, a restaurateur from Providence, Rhode Island. George and his wife, Johanne Killeen—the founders of Lucky's and Al Forno—were aficionados of cooking by fire; one night a steak had fallen through the grill and onto the smoldering charcoal embers, so they threw it aside and grilled a new one for the customer.

When the restaurant closed, the staff sliced up the steak and tried it, thinking "you never know."

Well, the crust was ethereal, the smokiness intoxicating. Rumor spread throughout the restaurant among diners who had heard the legend and started ordering this earthy, crusty creation.

Finally, after some time, the "Dirty Steak," as it came to be known, had to be retired.

As George once told me: "We were cooking so many of them, it put the fire out. So, we had to take it off the menu."

"We Took It Off the Menu"

(Half spoken, rubato)

No, I'm not gonna take any more of your lame excuses
But from now to quell your gastric juices
Oh, what in heaven's name will you do . . .
When you have to order something new?

WE TOOK IT OFF THE MENU
It got so hot we put the fire out
The kitchen door will not be open anymore
Not like before
No, not like before

We lost the secret recipe
Ran out of spice to kick up the intensity
We're at a loss to slowly concentrate the sauce
We just can't make it anymore

We used to live so high upon the hog
Living love so easily like falling off a log
But now we'll have to settle for
What we use the common kettle for . . .
A simple, decent stew
To sink our teeth into

Recall my dear how simply grand it was
But desire burns as fire often does
That slowly smoldering ember
Will become a flame no more
We just won't get it anymore

(Tag):
It will be a sad surprise
To see starvation in your eyes
My darling when you . . .
When you . . . Realize . . .

WE HAD TO TAKE IT OFF THE MENU
Bye, bye, baby . . . Bye Bye

An Electrifying, Upbeat Image to Close the Show

We needed a finale for SMOKE: *something up-tempo and brash, and that could be used as a duet. "You Electrify Me" is what came out. Lori Rivera would sing it as a solo in her initial* SMOKE *show, a brief sketch using an early script written by Kathryn Chetkovich. In a companion piece, written by Kathryn, Greg Fritsch and me, Juni Bucher did a separate, fifteen-minute sketch, singing different songs of love and deceit.*

For the finale, Juni and Lori joined forces to sing "Electrify Me" as the finale. Their powerful voices and stage presence brought the house down for the final "dessert course" set.

Several months later, I wrote a separate libretto (fine-tuned by both Greg and Kathryn), entitled Blowing Smoke. *It was about two male characters played by the same actor, one of them a sympathetic nice-guy bartender and the other a handsome lady-killer who comes into the bar on the make. The role was variously played by two local actors, Ralph Peduto and Durage Maxfield.*

And the beauty of the evening (in my opinion, at least) was that we were able to run all three SMOKE *shows—*SMOKE, Smoke Rings, *and* Blowing Smoke—*in sequence with all three actors performing the finale.*

"You Electrify Me"

I finally found what true romance is
You came around, I took my chances
You still astound me with your dances
For YOU ELECTRIFY ME

I follow you to foreign places
You leave a clue and I see only traces
Still I pursue your secret graces
For YOU ELECTRIFY ME

Justify me
Lustify me
Draw the line
As you define me
Rectify, objectify
ELECTRIFY ME

I'm always tricked by your disguises
Who could predict your sweet surprises?
The apple picked still tantalizes
'cause YOU ELECTRIFY ME

(Tag):
Rectify, objectify me . . .
Resurrect me . . . And protect me
Never fail me . . . Please e-mail me
Help perfect . . . Don't neglect me
You, you, E, E, E . . . Electrify me

Bop du dee da,
bop do da da
You, Ooo, Ooo
ELECTRIFY ME

Greg Needs Another Song!

Dear, dear, dear Greg—one of my major inspirations in our musical theater adventures—came to me one day and said we needed a love song/ballad for Celeste (played by Lori) for the end of SMOKE *to bring the story to a romantic close.*

"Another song? Oh, damn, Greg." I said, "It may look easy but it's not."

Greg smiled and said, "All you have to do is take 'Electrify Me' and change the lyrics a bit and turn it into a ballad. Easy."

Oh, yeah, I thought. You try it.

Of course, I refused. But a week later, I started to think: "How can I pull this off? You can't write a ballad with the rhythm of Da Da Da Da Da Da Da DA DA!"

So, I thought, "I'll have to drop out every other word. Maybe more."

When I saw Greg the next day, I said, "Give me a clue Greg, I don't even know where to start." He said, "You know. Use nice images like 'how you stir my tea.' That kind of stuff." (Notice the use of Greg's tea image in the second stanza. As I told him, "It's my line now." Just right.)

So, I attacked the challenge. For the title, I thought, I could use a play on "Electrify Me" and came up with "Intoxicate Me."

The lucky thing about the musical composition is that the chord progressions are identical, and in fact, if we ever need to stage a duet, both songs can be sung in counterpoint. We've never tried it, so I have no idea how it would sound.

"You Intoxicate Me"

How you do what you do
Sheer invention to me
You make up everything new
You do something to me

Utter magic you brew
Simply stirring my tea
You mix that potion, you do!
YOU INTOXICATE ME

You may not say but one word
But I drown myself in your story
I bask and glow in the glory
The glory of you . . . You and me

Guess I'll stay for a while
Hear your voice, see your smile
I drink in the moment with you
YOU INTOXICATE ME . . .

Songs From *Escaping Queens*—A Musical Memoir

Escaping Queens grew out of our success with *SMOKE* when I realized that Lori and I shared similar upbringings: a shiftless, drunken Puerto Rican father and a family having escaped New York for California. The original idea was that this one-woman show, *Latina,* would chart the childhood experiences of an abused daughter, using the monologue trope that worked so well in *SMOKE.*

Since the show began to take on the the length and scope of a fully staged musical, we decided to base the story on my memoir, *Pastina: My Father's Misfortune, My Mother's Good Soup.*

The show enjoyed two years of sold-out performances at Cabrillo Stage (2012 and 2013), having been accepted by artistic director Jon Nordgren.

For the sake of brevity, in this book, I decided not to include some of my other favorite tunes from *Escaping Queens:* "Another Woman," "AFew Moments of Magic," "Salsipuedes," and "Over the Roof." Look for them in a future compilation.

An Escape from Reality

My original experience of using fantasy to escape my parents' wild and crazy relationship was to imagine cowgirls like Marilyn Monroe and Rita Hayworth riding their "stallions" across the bedroom walls to help me fall asleep.

Since that image didn't fit into the Queens *storyline, Greg and I decided to change the image to cowboys. So, the song "Cowboy" was born, because Little Joey was so obsessed with Western movies and gun-toting heroes in anticipation of the family's escape to Southern California—and Hollywood.*

Both Greg and our musical director, Max Bennett-Parker, always felt it was perhaps my best composition. The song depicts the climax of child abuse that convinces Mama, once and for all, to kick her husband Herman out of the house for good, and hopefully conveys what any child might say to an abusive father.

"Cowboy"

Gonna ride on outta town
Sleep out under the stars
There won't be no more fences
Keepin' me from goin'

Listen to coyotes
Howlin' in the wind
Won't be no more bad guys
Trailin' after me

Ooooou, COWBOY
What you gonna do
Now that I'm standin' up to you?
Have some respect, mister
Spit that cig'rette out ya mouth
This time you'll be the one who's gettin' burned . . . Not me

>   Don't put your hand down by your gun
>   I'll take a stand, not gonna run (this time) . . . COWBOY
>   Don't put ya dukes up in my face
>   I'll drag your hide all over this place (this time) . . . COWBOY
>   If you lift your hand to me
>   You'll be surprised what you might see
>   Take your best shot . . . . Cowboy . . .
>   You know I will stand up to you
>   You won't believe what I can do (this time)

(spoken) What's wrong?

Cowboys don't cry
Cowboys get along
That's only dust in your eye . . . Cowboy . . . Don't cry

Gonna break outta this corral
It's so peaceful out on the range
Just me and the doggies and the moon

Now I gotta go
Kick that ol' campfire out
Get up on my horse and ride away . . .
COWBOY . . . Ride away

Songs from *Circus*

Greg and I had been ruminating about creating a "sung-through" musical (a musical in which the entire story is told in song) since our days at Michael's on Main, when he encountered two actors who couldn't deliver their lines effectively and decided to tell their story in actions, gestures, and song lyrics.

The show *Circus* was the result.

And again, our friend and supporter Jon Nordgren, then Artistic Director of Cabrillo Stage, signed us on to present the piece in the company's first outdoor Festival, in July 2021, just after Covid was starting to fade from our lives.

We got the sense that audiences were dumbfounded by a stage play delivered completely in song, but eventually—about midshow—they started to understand where the story was headed when they caught on to the operatic presentation. My other favorite tunes in the piece (not included here) are entitled "Rollercoaster Ride," "Season of No Reason," and "Wash Away."

Writing New Lyrics for an Existing Melody

It's fitting that "The Carnival Barker's Tune" almost creates a donut in this compilation, in that the original melody was poached from "Ragout"—the first song in the lyrics section of the book. I "replaced" the old lyric, as I had learned from songwriters like Irving Berlin, et al, by re-lyricizing an existing song to fit a new show and a new situation—simply the conniving song writer's attempt to showcase a melody he reveres as a personal favorite.

I needed a song the Carnival Barker uses to pull the crowd into his web with mesmerizing lingo—to convince them to pay a few pennies to see the human atrocities from which they, themselves, have been spared.

My original inspiration for this character, Paul Shenkman, a restaurateur from Half Moon Bay, once worked as a carnival barker in Atlantic City, beckoning the weak of spirit to enter in order to gain their own sense of personal redemption.

Welcome to this sideshow of human misery and be thankful for the wretched life fate has spared you.

The Carnival Barker's Tune:

(spoken)
Gather ye around me
Good Ladies and Gentle Men
Step into my dominion . . .
Of redemption and pain
Pay heed and you'll awaken
In wonder, hope and oft-shaken
Wisdom, where apparitions abound
To shock and astound

(singing):
Prepare to be bewildered
By what I'll show you
Of visions you'll see inside
The strange and the forsaken
Odd and sadly mis-shapened
Their loss—your salvation—
Arousing your pride

You'll see what will implore you
To test your spirit
Question your strength of will
Monstrosities that frighten
Indeed, will serve to enlighten
Your hope for good fortune
To assuage any ill

So, tell me what you want
I'll give you what you need
A bitter taste to taunt
Blind faith on which to feed
When darkness stokes your fear
Your gravest doubt will show
To hide what now comes clear
Where you pray you'll never go . . . *(continues on next page)*

Now, face your fears
Hold back your tears—
For their once and precious life
Mis-shaped by loss and strife
Open up your eyes
Be brave to view
The cruel and bitter joke
Which fate has spared of you!

WOMEN BEHIND THE CURTAIN -
(spoken):
He stands there on the midway
And lures believers
With mystery and lies
He summons their defiance
Stoking blind compliance
In bending the truth
With his words, smiles and eyes

CARNIVAL BARKER *(sings):*
Yes, I know what you want
A journey to the dark
Redemption from your fate
Your faithless sense of worth
You relish in the wounds
The fallen must endure
You, "The chosen" of the earth
In judgement of the poor

So, look and see
What the Almighty can bestow
Your fortune not to be
What you pray you'll never know
The mirror of your lives
When held up to your eyes
Intensifies the power of our show!

"Your Memory's a Thread if You're Willing to Pull"

The song "Rum, De Dumb, Dumb" was originally intended for a Kitchen Kabaret *sketch that never got produced. I had the crazy idea of a bottle of rum, strung on an invisible thread, dancing above the bar, singing to the bartender and playing with his mind in ridiculous and absurd rhymes. Well, we never could set up the apparatus to make the bottle fly above the bar, nor could I ever quite get the unwieldy lyrics to make sense in expressing the absurdity I was searching for.*

The Musical Circus *however, was the perfect production for the tune—expertly staged by Greg Fritsch and performed by the theater quadruple-threat (director, actor, singer, dancer), Andrew Ceglio.*

"Rum, De Dumb, Dumb"

One shot of courage needs two shots of rum
Forget why you came, to get high or get numb
Just roll the dice and the liars will come
The songs they won't sing but they'll hum

The clinking of glasses disguises your fear
And turns your regrets into swigs of good cheer
The booze tells a story you never may hear
You try to guess why you have come

> Only a sip is too much for some
> You look to the bottle to see why you've come
> You ask me to sing . . . but I only can hum
> RUM, DEE DUMB, DUMB, DEE DUMB DUMB

Sitting right next to you there in the dark
A ghost or an ember of some dying spark
It swears it won't touch you but still leaves its mark
If you buy it a drink it might come

The glass is half empty, the glass is half full
The past is a story that's loaded with bull
Your mem'ry's a thread if you're willing to pull
If you bargain or barter you've won . . . *(continues on next page)*

Only a sip is too much for some
You look to the bottle to see why you've come
You ask me to sing . . . but I only can hum
RUM, DEE DUMB, DUMB, DEE DUMB DUMB

Don't wave your drink or your secret might spill
Keep it held high so your soul you can fill
The liquid replaces the price of a pill
The cargo's the ship that comes in

So drink, so drink up, and don't think anymore
And scatter the bull, 'till you know it's for sure
Be careful your back isn't facing the door
Or you'll never know who might come in

So sit here and drink— Yes, and take it all in
The mem'ries won't sing but they'll hum
Rum dee dumb, dumb,
Dee dumb dumb, Dee dumb dumb
If rum brings no magic . . .
Try gin!

Some Tunes Take 50 Years to Write

In the early seventies I became enraptured by the music of bebop saxophonist Charles "Yardbird" Parker. So when my friend and former fraternity brother Phil Basile met his future wife, Chi Chi Chavez, I immediately recalled a "Bird" tune called Chi Chi. After many sessions at the piano plunking out the tune, I finally learned the melody and carried it in my memory, until eventually, I came up with a single-verse lyric that I also carried around mentally—in this case for five decades—stashed away in my mental file cabinet, never written down on paper.

Fast-forward 50 years: sitting around the piano with another friend, piano player Glen Rose, I asked him to play Parker's original chart for Chi Chi and sang him the lyrics to see if I could make them fit. Well, Glen went nuts and said, "What's the second verse?"

"That's all I got," I said. But, inspired by his response, I set out to finish the song and the second verse came to life. A few years later, when I was looking for a show to use the song in, I played a sample recorded version for Lori Rivera. When she heard it, she loved it and said, "I want to sing it."

I said, "You can't sing it, it's a guy's tune." Well, that didn't stop Lori. But a few days later I dug up the chart for another Charlie Parker composition called "Blues for Alice."

The miracle of miracles was that even though "Blues for Alice" was in a different key than "Chi Chi," with different chord changes, and with a different melody—because of the genius of "Bird"—these two "blues-extension" songs would fit over the same chord progression. I wrote the female lyrics for Lori based on the "Alice" melody, so the tune would become yet another argumentative exchange for a couple in the throes of a heated disagreement.

I never had an inkling that any political resonance could be attributed to the song, but after hearing Lori's recording of it (with local Santa Cruz talent Alex Lucero singing the male vocal part), I thought it might be something Don and Melania might use to wage war on one another.

And if you look carefully at the final two stanzas of Melania's verses, I think you'll agree.

"Melania's Tune"

DONALD:
If you would please give me your love
My heart would sail up to th'
All the way up to heaven above
I would be free
Free to hold you and to squeeze you
How I long to please you . . . CHI CHI
Take the baby, the Mercedes
and all your jewelry, and
Let's run off to Mexico,

You know that's where we'll go
We'll cruise down the highway
Trippin' along, it's my way, you know!
Just you and me (Oh, did I forget "Baby?")
Never mind, forgive me . . . CHI CHI
You attract me then distract me
I'm crazy you see
So, grab the keys, come on let's go!!!

MELANIA:
Go with me? Play with me?
You won't even stay with me,
While I'm in the room you must be
Smokin' a cigar or down at the bar
With a stranger, You act like such
A bigshot with no one you know!
So, all for show!
You don't take me anywhere
It complicates my groove
Prove me I'm wrong, (So) I'll play along!?!?

MELANIA (*continuing*)::
I've got the blues, lately
While you play it cool and stately
When I'm away you like to play,
Silly charades, plan lavish parades
With your voodoo

You practice all this sleight-of-hand,
Stand on a stage (It's) how you engage
Your magic tricks can never fix
What I see as wrong,
Why string along?
Why cling too long?

Sick mother, trick other
people in the audience
not me any more I've had it!
What am I here for?
Am I to endure without breaking?
You spend each waking moment
Stoking your brand, hiding your hand
The curtain that you stand behind must
Hide what's locked inside
Tell me I'm wrong (So) I'll string along!!!

(*ENDING TAG, in call and response*):

HIM:	HER:
Come on you know you wanna	The hell I will
Go with me . . . Off to Tijuana!!!	Another dive motel in TJ?
You and Me	No way, Jose!
Come on you know you wanna	Dream on
Go with me	I'll pass, thank you
And don't forget baby	It was a Beemer, you idiot

Both: CHI CHI

Acknowledgements

Thanks to:

Nils Peterson – for the first inspiration of writing poetry at San Jose State College.

Kathryn Chetkovich – for dramaturgy, script consultations, and numerous libretti.

Greg Fritsch – for support in all five of our musical theater ventures.

Gayle – for life inspiration and support, and for designing the cover.

Lori Rivera – for inspiration in seeing the female vision in song lyrics.

Bonnie Ronzio – for many years of stage management and devotion.

Glen Rose – for accompanist sessions on piano in charting tunes.

Max Bennett-Parker – for musical direction in several productions.

Jon Nordgren – for the three productions he offered us at Cabrillo Stage.

Maggie Paul – for poetry editing and inspiration.

Sarah Rabkin – for reading and editing the anecdotal song histories and galley proof.

Michael Seal Riley – *Style Magazine* editor par excellence.

Stuart Kestenbaum – for the wonderful poetry workshop at Shakerag, 2023.

Amber Shaw – for help with self-publication.

Steve McGuirk – for convincing me to "dive into ink."

Jana Marcus – for publicist work on *Escaping Queens* and the poster on page 62.

www.ingramcontent.com/pod-product-compliance
Lightning Source LLC
Chambersburg PA
CBHW020334130626
46549CB00003B/1171